# HOW TO START A CRASHPAD –Turn Your Mortgage into Cash Utilizing The Airline Industry

By Tara Sky

# Copyright

Copyright © 2017 by Tara Sky

All rights reserved. No part of this publication may be reproduced, distributed, or transmitted in any form or by any means, including photocopying, recording, or other electronic or mechanical methods, without the prior written permission of the author, except in the case of brief quotations embodied in critical reviews and certain other noncommercial uses permitted by copyright law. For permission requests, write to the author, addressed "Attention: Permissions Coordinator," at the address below.

Tara Sky
crashpadqueen.com

Version 2.2

# Dedication

*I dedicate this book to everyone else who dreams of early retirement. You got this!*

*This book is also dedicated to my husband, Angel, who made this book possible through his everlasting support, creative genius and love.*

## How to Start and Manage a Crash Pad
## Table of Contents

# Contents

**COPYRIGHT** ................................................................. 1

**DEDICATION** ................................................................ 2

**PREFACE** .................................................................... 4

**ACKNOWLEDGEMENTS** ................................................ 8

**CRASH PAD 101** ......................................................... 9

**CHAPTER 1: HEAD IN THE CLOUDS** ........................... 11
    REVIEW AND APPLICATION ............................................. 14

**CHAPTER 2: PLANTING MY FEET** ............................... 15
    CREATE A FOUNDATION AND IDENTIFY YOUR RESOURCES. ....... 15
    REVIEW AND APPLICATION ............................................. 19

**CHAPTER 3: MARKET RESEARCH** ............................... 20
    REVIEW AND APPLICATION ............................................. 24

**CHAPTER 4: ORGANIZATION IS KEY!** ......................... 25
    CALCULATE EVERYTHING. ............................................... 25
    LABELING! ................................................................. 27
    ORGANIZATIONAL DOCUMENTS! ...................................... 27
    BILLING! .................................................................... 30
    REVIEW AND APPLICATION ............................................. 31

**CHAPTER 5: MARKETING & SOCIAL NETWORKING** ...... 32
    GIVE YOUR CRASH PAD A NAME! ..................................... 32
    VISUAL APPEAL! ......................................................... 33
    SOCIAL MEDIA! .......................................................... 33
    NETWORK, NETWORK, NETWORK! .................................. 33
    CHECK IN! ................................................................. 34

 Respond to Your Potential Clients! ........................................ 37
 Referrals & Reviews! ................................................................ 37
 Review and Application ............................................................ 39

## CHAPTER 6: THE APPLICATION PROCESS ........................ 41
 1. Candidate applies. ............................................................... 41
 2. Touch base with the Candidate (Informal Interview). ............................................................................... 42
 3. Check References. ............................................................... 44
 4. Invoice & Agreement. .......................................................... 45
 5. Collect Money & Signed Agreement. ................................ 46
 The Agreement. ....................................................................... 47
 Review and Application ............................................................ 55

## CHAPTER 7: YOU WILL FAIL ................................................... 56
 Identify your failures (or need for improvement). .............. 56
 Address your failures, devise a plan, and execute. ........... 57
 Feedback and Reviews. ......................................................... 57
 Celebrate Your Successes! .................................................... 59
 Review and Application ............................................................ 60

## CHAPTER 8: TRANSPORTATION .......................................... 62
 Community Car. ..................................................................... 62
 On Call Shuttle Driver. ........................................................... 64
 Public Transportation. ........................................................... 66
 Review and Application ............................................................ 67

## CHAPTER 9: CLIENT RELATIONS ......................................... 68
 Keep Your Clients at a Distance! .......................................... 68
 Avoid Living in the Crash Pad. .............................................. 70
 Don't Allow Crashers to Live in the Crash Pad. .................. 71
 Bad Apples. ............................................................................. 72
 Feedback & Word of Mouth! ................................................. 73
 Review and Application ............................................................ 74

## CHAPTER 10: QUALITY OF CRASH PAD LIFE ..................... 76

| | |
|---|---|
| SECURITY. | 76 |
| SET UP. | 76 |
| ATMOSPHERE. | 78 |
| WEEKLY HOUSEHOLD RESPONSIBILITIES. | 80 |
| YOUR MAINTENANCE TEAM. | 81 |
| REVIEW AND APPLICATION | 83 |

**CHAPTER 11: MONEY MATTERS ......................................................... 85**

| | |
|---|---|
| MONEY MATTERS. | 85 |
| SEASONS. | 86 |
| REPORTING INCOME. | 87 |
| BACK-UP PLAN. | 88 |
| INVEST WISELY! | 90 |
| REVIEW AND APPLICATION | 92 |

**ABOUT THE AUTHOR ............................................................................ 93**

# Preface

All I ever wanted was to travel the world, have a couple of children, live comfortably and retire early. The road to achieving these aspirations have proven to be more authentic than I had ever imagined. I'm on my way. Executive director of a chain of crash pads at age thirty-two, I've proudly earned both of these titles in the last five years and I am excited to share my story with you!

But let's face it, my life has always been funny, different, interesting. The off-beaten path has always drawn me in, and this brings about so many adventures that most people never dare to embrace. And I love it, thrive on it even.

I think that this was ingrained in me as a child. When I mention that my parents divorced when I was three, most people say in pity, "I'm sorry, that must have been hard." My reply is "*Hard?* Listen, I had two birthdays and two Christmases every year. I was both the baby of the family *and* my Dad's only child. My parents got along when it came to parenting me. I had it pretty good!" Even then, I remember how lucky I felt to have two completely different lives. I was homeschooled until seventh grade. This taught me the lesson of working hard so you can play harder. After buckling down and completing my lessons for the week, I would spend the next three days building Barbie towns, playing never-ending Monopoly games and filming commercials about the mud pies I had freshly baked with my sisters. I must have seemed so confused as a junior high student, floating between all of the "clicks" on a daily basis. One day, I would wear Wranglers and spend time with the "kickers". The next, I would borrow my sister's JNCO's to fit in with the "bangers". I had preppy clothes too, but the "preps" always seemed to be the most exclusive of all of the groups, and as a result, I pulled away from them a bit more. Still, I enjoyed mingling with all the types, and I found there was something to learn from everyone, and that while the clothes we wore were different, there was something inside all of us that connected us all the same.

I fell in love with the French language and culture on my first day of high school. For my following birthday, I asked for a French exchange student. Two study abroad programs later, I decided to major in French. "Why aren't you learning Spanish?" they all said... "You're not going to use French in the South!" *They were right!* I wasn't going to use French in the southern U.S., and I needed to go far, far away to utilize the language to my fullest advantage. *So what did I do?* On my eighteenth birthday, I got a tattoo of the French flag on my back, and after completing college in three years, I joined the Peace Corps. Cameroon taught me the importance of community, the unimportance of material possessions, and allowed me to discover the rewards of helping others. I learned how to manage projects and to make things happen, regardless of the obstacles that were thrown my way. My time in the Peace Corps provided me with much more than I was ever able to provide to others: resilience, a full heart, knowing that I can make a difference, and the eagerness to do more. I adored my life as a foreigner adapting to a new culture, and ever since returning to the states, the only way I can describe the feeling I had was *stuck*. Not that I didn't enjoy being closer to family and planting some roots; I just couldn't shake the travel bug that had bitten me. With the contacts I had made in Cameroon, I started a nonprofit organization and was able to travel back to Cameroon to provide solar panels to an orphanage. All the while, I was teaching French at a private school. I decided to start a fair trade lingerie business that ultimately failed after a house fire (and an engagement) that went up in flames.

Yes, all my hard work and investment went up in smoke! After raising more than $15,000 to launch the business through an Indiegogo campaign, I spent six weeks in Cameroon working with local women to design and create our first batch of inventory. I returned to the states with more bags than I could carry, to a very broken relationship with my co-founder and fiancé, and an empty house. I awoke at 2:00 A.M. to the sound of the fire alarm. Looking back, I can only laugh at the literal metaphor of walking into my living room to see a picture of us from our first date on the end table, slowly burning up in orange flames. Another fun fact: I was sleeping in the nude. In my frantic shock, I grabbed the first thing I saw, a woven maize bag, and started slapping at the fire with no result. The fire had originated underneath the vent on the floor, making it impossible to put it out. Again, in shock, I wrapped that same bag around me after throwing my puppy outside, before running to the neighbors' house. As I sat half-naked in the yard with my arms around my dog, my hair still woven into braids and smelling of Africa, I watched the flames swallow my dreams. I cried hysterically for all of the women whose lives I wanted to impact, whose donations I wished had counted for something, and for all of the hard work I had invested into those products.

When the journalist interviewed me at 4:00 A.M., I told her that all I could do is be thankful that we got out safe, and that I had faith that everything happens for a reason.

I tell you this story because these experiences have certainly been for a reason, and my success has not come without sacrifice nor has it come without learning bits and pieces of how to run a business, how to lean on my faith, and how to dust yourself off and push forward when you find yourself at the bottom. Furthermore, I thank my mother for passing on to me a creative, dreaming mind full of ideas, and I thank my dad for giving me the drive, stubbornness and work ethic to bring some of those ideas to life. Thanks to their support and love, I always knew I could fly. Life is a series of events, compiled together, and these details have led me to this point.

I hope that by sharing my experiences, you will get a laugh or a chuckle out of my stories of crash pad life and that you will be inspired to pursue a dream that maybe you've feared taking on thus far. If you are considering starting a crash pad, I hope that by sharing the lessons I have learned you will be more adequately prepared to start one. Or, if by the end of this book, you decide that running a crash pad isn't for you, then I will be grateful to have saved you from taking flight to somewhere you didn't really want to visit in the first place.

## Acknowledgements

I would like to thank my Dad for his undivided support and unconditional love, from beautiful childhood memories, moving to Africa, buying a house, to fixing ceiling fans. I have only come this far because of you!

Thank you, my dearest friend, Mr. Sminu Peter! Thanks for picking up the phone at 2 AM while my house was burning up and my life was falling apart, and for celebrating with me when life built me up again. And then you agreed to be my editor, without even knowing how many commas you would have to slash, and critiqued my first written baby with the most delicate care. *Thank you.*

Finally, my heart overflows with gratitude for my husband, my best friend, my partner in life, Angel. Thank you for believing in me. Thank you for your help, whenever I've needed it, for listening to my wandering ideas, and for contributing and supporting me with your whole heart. And especially for the formatting and beautiful cover design of my first book! I'm so proud of us and I can't wait to spend the rest of my life with you!

# Crash Pad 101

*Let's start with the basics and get familiar with a few terms.*

**Webster's Dictionary defines CRASH PAD as the following:**
**1:** protective padding (as on the inside of an automobile or a tank)
**2:** a place to stay temporarily

For an airline crew member (such as a flight attendant or a pilot), a crash pad is a place to stay temporarily, in between flight sequences, located at the crew member's base (chosen by the airline, not the crew member). A crash pad provides a place to sleep, eat, and shower when needed. It replaces a hotel and requires a monthly cost, usually cheaper than what one would spend on a hotel. Crash pads are temporary, and in most cases require only month to month contracts.

**Crasher**: Someone who pays monthly in return for a place to stay temporarily, not to reside permanently. Many airline crew members become crashers, as they commute from their home which is not located at their base city (or hub).

**Hot Bed**: A bed shared by more than one person and is used on a first-come-first-serve basis. Hotbeds are usually offered at a cheaper rate than dedicated beds.

**Private (Cold) Bed**: A bed dedicated to only one individual, for one person's use.

**Reserve**: A schedule given to flight attendants and pilots, making them available to the company for a given amount of time. Some airlines provide straight reserve schedules to crew, meaning that they are constantly on call (and thus, will spend more time at their crash pad).

**Line month:** A schedule of flight sequences (or work trips) given to crew who are senior enough to hold them. This usually allows for more flexibility, and in turn, means that crew holding a line will spend significantly less time at their crash pad.

# Chapter 1: Head in the Clouds

After teaching French at a private school for two years, I jumped at the opportunity to become a flight attendant when I found that a major airline was hiring. I packed up my faith and took off to training for eight and a half weeks.

Eight and a half weeks of hell, or "Barbie Boot Camp" as they call it. After the Peace Corps, I took on the belief that I could do anything, go anywhere, and succeed. Training made me question that belief every day. We were tested multiple times per week, we ran through drills over and over, and we were constantly graded on appearance and attitude. Things I never gave much thought to became a way of life. Wearing lipstick and high heels became a priority, and we could be sent away from class for hair wispies getting out of line. I stocked up on the *"extra hold"* hairspray and should have bought stock in pantyhose. Much like a reality TV show, we were being watched all the time. From the cafeteria ladies to the hotel staff, we were always on guard and trying to make the very best impression, which was utterly exhausting. There were even rumors that there were microphones in the salt and pepper shakers, and that the hotel provided security camera footage to the training staff. To make matters worse, our lead instructor, Ed, was more or less a ninja with a temper. The invisible eyes in the back of his head saw **everything**, and he demanded perfection from us. His love was tough, so tough that I couldn't tell you how many times he made me cry that summer. I was so nervous and anxious to succeed, to begin with. From the first time I failed an exam, I spiraled into more failure that led me into a funk, which in turn, made me less confident. I became more anxious by week six, which I like to refer to as *hell week*.

Which is why I paid no attention to Angel when we took the shuttle back to the hotel together. He chatted me up about his birthday, and we discovered we were both Leos. Then he told me that he was going out *dancing* and that he had been going out *soooo* much since he had been in Dallas. "Going out?!" I thought. After the training day, practicing drills and studying for next days' exams, I could hardly stay awake long enough for Netflix with my roommate. Angel was not only *going out all the time*, but he was also running a website business on the side and seemed to be frolicking his way through training. I silently cursed Angel, just having completed week three, "*Just wait* until he gets to hell week!"

Training was a dark place for me. And somewhere along the way, I saw the flight attendant pay scale. I knew that I wouldn't be making millions, but I certainly wasn't expecting wages less than teacher salary. I learned that for the greater part of our career, we wouldn't be getting paid! Not for signing into the airport an hour prior to departure, checking our emergency equipment, setting up the meals and beverage carts, delays... not even for boarding! I was disappointed, but at the same time, money wasn't the only goal here. The goal was doing a job that I loved, seeing the world, and making millions in the equivalent of the free flights I would have.

I didn't even know what a crash pad was. I had heard the term thrown around a couple of times, and one day some of the girls who flew previously started discussing it in class. I quickly became very curious. "Where are these crash pads?" I asked. They told me that they were located near airports in base cities and that, most of the time, they were cheap apartments. Crew members needed them so that they had a place to sleep just before and after their flight sequences since they commuted from where they lived, and where they lived did not have a base. "What's the typical pay to stay in a crash pad?" "About two-hundred-and-fifty dollars", they told me. "And how many people usually share a crash pad?" One of the girls gasped, "I've heard of one particular crash pad that had *nineteen* people crashing in a two bedroom apartment!" Now, I'm not the greatest at math, but it didn't take me long to realize just how much profit could be made here. It wasn't a difficult decision to decide that I wanted to start a crash pad. On top of my itch to run a business again, I wanted to *own* something, to have an investment, and was going to need all the help I could get to pay a mortgage. Now that my head was going to be in the clouds with my new career, it seemed like the perfect time to plant my feet on the ground.

## Review and Application

*Before making the commitment to start a crash pad, please consider the following carefully.*

**So you want to start a crash pad...?**
1. Why do you want to start and manage a crash pad?
2. What previous experience do you have that has equipped you with what it takes to successfully manage a crash pad?
    a. Do you have a support network that will help you with certain aspects of running a crash pad (such as maintenance, marketing, accounting, and technology)?
3. Are you ready for the work, time, and responsibility it takes to run a crash pad?
4. What information do you have about crash pad supply and demand in your area?

# Chapter 2: Planting My Feet

*Create a foundation and identify your resources.*

After surviving and graduating from training, I became a full-on flight attendant! I was assigned my base and was ready to plant my feet. I began my hunt for the perfect house.

But let me back up and give my Dad a shout out for having my back every step of the way. Sometimes we don't even realize the sacrifices people make for us until we are mature enough to understand it; a love that goes so deep and stretches so far, that there's no way you could ever doubt that love for one second. That love nourished me with the support I needed to complete training and gave me everything I needed to form a foundation for a crash pad.

And remember hell week, and the over-confident, boasting guy cruising through training that I shared a shuttle with? I knew his heart was big when he became the first contributor to the Haiti mission trip I was fundraising for, but when he asked me out to dance one Saturday evening, I took a chance. He opened up my heart, wider than I thought I would ever be able to again. He restored hope and faith I felt I had long lost, and became a beautiful piece of the puzzle that I needed to create the framework for my success as a crash pad manager. An extensive background in building websites, social marketing and media, and business management, Angel quickly became my assistant manager. It became a great benefit to both of us because he was happy to provide the help for nothing in return, except my love. He's become an irreplaceable piece of my puzzle to success, with every technology solution, every trash bag taken to the curb, and every word of encouragement I ever needed to hear when things became too difficult.

I was determined to own a house by the end of the year, and here I was in October. Nothing was stopping me...except my income. Although my credit was excellent (may I take a moment to boast about the fact that I have *never* made a late payment and always pay my bills in full), the loan officer explained to me that without more security than the 75 hour-per-month guarantee, I wouldn't be able to afford a place that I could actually convince crew members to stay at. I could have rented a house, sure. But this would have created a difficult situation, having to consider a landlord's permission before starting a crash pad within a rental. I had already heard horror stories about crash pad managers who set themselves up at a rental, only to be shut down when their landlord found out. It was not a risk I was willing to take, and furthermore, I was thinking more about long-term profit here, where the end result was to own a house in the first place. At that point, my hopes for the crash pad were that they would simply help me pay my mortgage, and I expected nothing more than that. After several long discussions, my Dad gracefully offered to combine his credit with mine, and the search began.

Melanie, my realtor, and I met at a Starbucks one morning and discussed what I was looking for: A house with as many rooms as possible, a large yard for the dog, one-story preferred, close to the airport. I was hoping to find a house located just off the transportation line. I would later learn that transportation was the *most important factor* in setting up my crash pad.

That same day I met with Melanie, she led me to the house that took my breath away. Upon entering the house, I fell in love with the hardwood floors, high ceilings and unique "L" shape that made me feel as if I was in a royal compound, hidden away from all society- and yet so very close to the airport! The previous owners even left a canopy covered patio set that overlooked the huge yard, filled with luscious trees and a vintage fountain. I discovered large bedrooms and one enclosed dining room, which I easily transformed into an additional bedroom in my mind. I estimated how many beds I could comfortably fit within the house. The master bedroom sealed the deal, and the master bathroom was *the cherry on top*. "You could have an orgy in the shower!" Melanie exclaimed. Not only did the enclosed shower contain two shower heads, but there was a jet tub featured *within* the shower as well. I laughed, looked at Melanie and said, "I can't afford this house!" She told me to guess how much the owners were asking for it. I was never more thrilled to be wrong.

Without boring you too much over the details of buying a house, let's just say that our offer was accepted, and on November 7th, 2013, exactly one year after the house fire, I became a homeowner!

# Review and Application

*Consider your foundation, the springboard for which to start and manage your crash pad.*

**Create a foundation and identify your resources.**
1. If you don't have a house, do you have the credit to buy one?
2. If not, do you have a parent or family member that may serve as a co-lender to help you purchase a house?
3. It is possible to rent a house to make into a crash pad, however, keep in my mind that your landlord might not allow it (check the lease).
4. Do you know anyone that may be able to contribute, and who you get along with well?
    a. Will you compensate that person(s) for their time?
5. How will you address and manage the transportation needs of the crash pad?

# Chapter 3: Market Research

*Research it. Talk about it! Ask questions, and listen carefully to those who are doing what you are trying to do!*

As a former business owner and entrepreneur, I knew that I needed to gather all the information I could get, and ask all the questions I could about running a crash pad. And who better to discuss my ideas with than my fellow colleagues, who might have a need for one, or had experience staying at one? I brainstormed the plan with whoever would listen, and when I wasn't talking about it, my journal served as a perfect soundboard. I googled twin bed measurements, and I drew out floor plans and designs for the house. I made a list of ideas to market the crash pad. placing "word of mouth" at the top of the list, knowing that this would be my most profitable marketing tool. Hence, I set out to make it the very best. A fellow crew member connected me with Jose, a flight attendant who manages a nineteen-person, all male crash pad in Miami and who only flies for fun. I picked his brain and jotted down his responses on a notepad as if I were cramming for a final exam. He seemed surprised and displeased that my mother and I would be living there as well. "Create separate spaces," he encouraged me, "and remember that the crashers will be your clients, not your friends." He told me that he has a maid who cleans bi-weekly and takes out the trash. *We'll save money there,* I figured, between my mother and myself. He advised me to purchase used, wood bunk beds because they are sturdy and don't make so much squeaking noise. He urged me to keep a constant waitlist so that I could always keep it full. "What about transportation?" I inquired. He replied, "My crash pad is located on the bus line. Other crash pads have cars - just a beater car that the crashers are responsible for putting gas into. They figure that out on their own." He added that his crashers provide their own bedding as well, but otherwise, the place pretty much runs itself. Lastly, he urged me to set expectations with a list of rules that must be followed by the crashers and to include that crashers may not move furniture around without the owner's permission. To this day, I'm still not sure what story stands behind that rule, but I made sure to write it into my agreement, per his recommendation.

**Research what exists in your area already, what those crash pads offer their clients, and how much they cost. What can you offer? This will allow you to see who you're competing with, and to decide on a price for your product.**

I perused the bulletin boards and scrolled through the profiles on CrashPad411.com, which featured apartments for the area. I knew I would have an advantage in offering a home environment. I didn't notice that any particular pad stood out with logos or professional photography. Prices ranged from $150-$250 monthly. Some crash pads offered hotbeds, which I quickly learned were not ideal for me. Hotbeds allow crashers to share a bed with one or more people at a lower rate, but if they happen to arrive after the bed's been taken, they must sleep on the floor or on an air mattress. I wanted to offer a private space and to have a smaller number of people coming in and out of my home. I also wanted everyone to form relationships with the rest of the community. Each client would rest assured that their bed was their space and that they could leave whatever they wanted there with it. I would be offering private beds, equipped common areas and a large, peaceful backyard, as well as shuttle service and a breakfast bar, to sweeten the deal even more. I decided on $250 for the going rate at my pad. After several months, when the spots within the house were almost full, I raised the cost to $260 per month for new crashers.

**Consider offering a discount at the beginning.**

At first, I offered discounts for six-month and one-year contracts (*"extended stays"*), so that an incentive would be available for the crasher to pay less while creating less work for me if that person stays for a longer period. I tried some other discounts, such as allowing the first month free, but it attracted girls who were looking to strike at the opportunity, and they would leave fairly quickly once the discount wasn't offered to them anymore. What I sometimes do is provide a 25% New Hire discount, or provide 25% off for referrals, showing those applicants that I want to help them out some and work with them. I find that overall, however, the more heavily you discount your product, the less value your clients will give your product.

**Make a list of what your market needs, and decide how you plan to accomplish meeting those needs.**

I knew that my market would be mostly females, and because of the type of environment I wished to create, decided that I would limit my crash pad to women only. I knew that they would appreciate an additional space to prep those lips and tips, so I would create an Image Room with which the girls could use, aside from the bathrooms. I knew that I would need lots of bunk beds, so I researched the going rate for sturdy bunk beds and mattresses. My crashers would need transportation, too. I made lists upon lists within my journal, which helped me to keep my thoughts organized, as well as address my questions with solutions as they came up. Moreover, I proposed those questions with crew who had used a crash pad in the past, and carefully considered every two cents that was thrown my way.

# Review and Application

*Now it's time to research and gather information! This will allow you to compete in the market.*

1. **Research the answers to your questions!**
    a. Do you have connections within the airline in which you can talk to about what the needs are, and can help connect you to your market?
    b. Talk about your idea with everyone, and listen to tips and advice that is offered (and read the rest of this book!).
2. **What exists in your area already?**
    a. What is the local pricing for crash pads?
    b. What do you think is a fair monthly price for your crash pad?
    c. What do they offer vs. what you can offer?
    d. Will you offer private beds or hotbeds?
3. **Make a list of your market needs, and decide how to address them.**
    a. Create lists of questions and details (such as bunk beds, vanity for an image room, etc. etc.) that you will need to consider.
    b. What about transportation?
    c. Talk to everyone, and listen to every two cents! You may get some great ideas!

# Chapter 4: Organization is Key!

***Calculate Everything.***

After spending a day with the measuring tape, a calculator, a pen, and paper, we decided to organize our first crash room to fit three bunk beds *or six girls*. Now, had we had the finances to invest then, it would have been ideal to install custom-built bunk beds with shelves, but we didn't have the startup capital. We purchased our first wood bunk beds from Ikea but later found even sturdier ones for sale on Craigslist. I became a very good Craigslist scout, although there are *If This Than That* recipes which can help you narrow your search, and will email you an alert when what you're looking for becomes available. I called around the area for the best deals on the best twin mattresses, and found a store that refurbishes mattresses- by far the best price in town! They even delivered them in bulk for a reasonable fee.

We bought wood numbers, spray-painted them pink, and wood-glued them onto their corresponding beds. This helped us significantly as we grew, from our *Projections* spreadsheet to communicating with crashers *what* bunk we were referring to when we were away. We eventually installed brackets, so that names could be written on a notecard and dropped into the metal frame; This reflects who reserves that bed, or who will be coming in to *move into* that bed if I can't be present to personally welcome that crasher.

I regret that we did not do all the above sooner. In our beginning months one of our original crashers, Lisa, had told us that she would be moving out in the middle of the month. A new client with the same name would be moving in as soon as a different spot was available, and another girl would be coming into Lisa's spot when the bed opened up. One of our other crashers left the crash pad a few days earlier than expected, and in an effort to accommodate everyone, we invited the same named girl to move in a few days before at no additional cost. Having mixed up Lisa's spot with the *other* girls', one girl came home one night and found another sleeping in her bed. I didn't find out about it until late, as I was in Mexico with limited connection. It was a mess, especially since one of the girls came at the other aggressively, with an attitude- cussing up a storm, threatening one of our most senior crashers, (how it was even *her fault*, I don't know why) and waking everyone else up in the process -and other beds were open, where she could have slept until we figured it out in the morning. Girls were upset, I had to have several uncomfortable conversations the following day, and I didn't enjoy my Mexico layover very much. I feared that it would be the end of our great reputation. *Hard lessons learned: Stay organized. Check and double-check who's assigned to each bed, physically throughout the crash pad and marked on the Projections excel spreadsheet. Keep it simple by requiring all crashers to pay through the end of each month in which they occupy a spot. Don't fall over backward trying to accommodate* everyone. <u>Require references</u> in the application process, to avoid another "hot mess" crasher that we kicked out after her three day stay with us.

We blocked off a space in the corner of our long dining room and converted it into the *Image Room*. I obtained an affordable, elegant vanity on Craigslist, purchased a pink, full-length mirror, and hung some organizer baskets on the wall, containing bobby pins, hairspray, and a hairdryer. This offered a space where girls could get ready if they had an early sign-in, without waking the other girls, and an additional prep area if both bathrooms were ever occupied. One of our current crashers is uncomfortable changing in front other crashers, so this provides an additional private space to accommodate her as well.

*The Dollar General* provided us with affordable caddies that we numbered and organized in a cabinet where they fit comfortably. This provided a specific space for each crasher, according to whatever bunk they occupied. We learned just how important these were when, as we expanded, we had noticed copious amounts of shampoo and conditioner bottles, razors, washcloths & lotions, in and around the showers. This also made it possible for girls to use whichever bathroom is available when they need it since their things would no longer be attached to just one bathroom.

These are just some of the things we considered. No doubt that your crash pad will come with its own set of challenges, and creating ways around how to face them early on will significantly save you time, money and complaints.

## **Labeling!**

Can you see how important labels are yet? After constant questioning of *"where's this thing and that thing?"* by every new crasher, we bought a label maker from Amazon, and one of our crashers gladly went to town on the kitchen (refrigerator included) and laundry room, claiming it to be *"an OCD wet dream"* upon completion. This proved to eliminate confusion on where things like the iron, pots & pans, and detergent are to be placed, as well as to what items could be tossed out, since judging by their labeled bunk correlation, we knew they belonged to *so-and-so*, and if *so-and-so* had left the crash pad, the items could then become community items, or thrown away, if items were completely undesirable.

We posted signs around the house, reminding crashers to be quiet and courteous to others as they moved about the house, and to wash, dry and put away their dishes immediately upon use.

We have since started providing freezer labels, which can be marked on and stored on food items within the refrigerators.

We've also learned how valuable a strict policy for belongings at the crashpad is. We have implemented the rule that every crasher must label each box/container of belongings, as well as hangers in the closet. My biggest reason for this is safety- to leave floor space within all the rooms open. This promotes tidiness and cleanliness within the crash pad environment as well.

## *Organizational Documents!*

At the time, I purchased a small metal filing cabinet, some hanging filing folders, and some manila folders. I created a hanging folder, titled *Clients*, and created a folder for each crasher as they made their deposit with us. There, we placed their signed agreement. *Now* we are completely digital, and I recommend you go paperless too! Here are the following systems I use to organize our documents:

**Google Documents**: We use Google Docs for notes, letters, and signs.

**Google Forms**: We use Google Forms as our application form to collect the necessary information to process. The form spits out the information into an Excel spreadsheet that then serves as an organizational tool. This form is also convenient to the bed registry, bed change request form, Referral form, Maintenance, and Supplies Request form and Notice of Vacancy form. Up until recently, we even used the Google Form as a way for new clients to sign their agreement online.

We designed a **Projections Excel Spreadsheet**, where we keep record of current clients, the bed they occupy, and at what rate they pay for their bunk. For each month, there are blanks where expenses are entered. We carefully created the document to calculate gross and net profits, so that we can keep track of every detail.

### *Billing!*

My favorite day of the month is the first because this is the day that our labor and efforts are converted into money! We accept payments via direct bank deposit, Venmo, and PayPal. Both Paypal and Venmo are convenient, instant and free to use anywhere when the account is linked to a checking account. We used to accept checks and cash, but given the amount of time, I spend traveling and honestly created more work just to retrieve those payments. We removed the hanging deposit boxes and now operate completely remotely- and it works well for everyone!

We learned quickly that having a place where we could keep record of our income would be crucial to tracking our progress, and making sure that every client was paying the amount that was agreed to be paid when it's supposed to be paid! We set up a billing system called Pancake Invoicing App (but there are lots of options out there), in which clients can access their invoices and receipts online, and where reminders are sent out to remind clients before payments are due. This system will also add on a fee to cover the extra charge should the client use a credit card (I really hate paying fees, so I love this feature!).

After the first of each month, I sit down and verify that all of my clients have paid the agreed upon amounts, and mark their invoices as paid. I then double check that all of my invoices for the next month are set up and ready to go. Of course, sometimes things change within a month, and things happen that call for modifying invoices- but the more organized we are with the billing, the more smoothly everything runs. Deposit is required to reserve a bed and prorated rent amounts should be due and paid before the client first arrives to the crashpad.

There's one last detail I really enjoy doing every month, after invoices have been marked as paid, and everything is set up to go for the following month. I check my projections sheet against the invoices for the correct amounts, I note the expenses for that month, and my excel calculations provide the net profits, or the income we have earned after the necessary expenses have been covered. I like to compare the months to each other, and consider details that could help us improve that figure for the following month. I have found this to be the best strategy, as crash pads are month to month businesses. This is the beauty of it, and this is also the uncertainty and risk of it. If for one month, the profits aren't so notable, there's always next month. It's a rolling process: Keep the spots within your spreadsheet filled, and the rates in line with demand in your area, while maintaining the happiness & satisfaction of your clients. And at the end of the day, or month in this case, always count the fruits of your labor!

# Review and Application

*Organization is everything! Your life will be easier with the provided tips, we promise!*

1. **Calculate Everything.**
    a. Measure everything out and decide how your layout will be. Decide on a goal for how many crashers you would like to start with.
    b. Will you be able to afford custom-built bunks, or will you purchase bunk beds?
    c. Don't forget to price and order your mattresses!
    d. Create a Projections Spreadsheet, and decide how you would like to organize your beds (We named the rooms, numbered the beds, and hung chalkboards where the names of crashers were to be written in)!
    e. Decide where and how you will provide a storage space (caddies? Cabinets in the kitchen?).
2. **Label everything!**
    a. Label bunks, storage spaces, and anything new crashers may need to find within the crash pad.
    b. Post important rules around the pad.
3. **Organize Your Documents!**
    a. Organize and save client documents and contracts.
    b. Maintain your Projections spreadsheet!

4. **Set Up Your Billing!**
    a. Maintain convenient payment methods and a billing system that clients can easily access, and where you can easily record how much revenue is coming in.
    b. Set aside one day every month to double check that payments were made.
    c. Check these figures with your Projections spreadsheet!

# Chapter 5: Marketing & Social Networking

### *Give your crash pad a name!*

To run my crash pad as a business, I needed to choose a memorable name that would stand out and let crew know that we are professional. After a lot of brainstorming, I decided on a name that intertwined airline lifestyle with luxury living, a soft place to rest one's head, and a part of the property address!

### *Visual Appeal!*

Angel contributed his talents to create a website and a Facebook group. He designed a lovely logo that would surely appeal to our female audience, but you can hire artists on UpWorks or similar websites. We designed flyers that we posted in every *Flight Operations* area within the airport and training center. We ordered business cards that highlighted our amenities and contained our contact info.

### *Social Media!*

Angel created a beautiful website where potential candidates could get an idea of what we offer, our amenities, and our location. The website included a form in which prospective clients could send us their information as well. We set up our profile on Crashpad411 and Facebook, and we created a slideshow set to some happy music, which we then posted on our website and Facebook profile. We made efforts to post images and events on our Facebook, as well as notifications of new openings within the crash pad. There are tons of Facebook crashpad specific groups where you will want to have a presence.

## Network, Network, Network!

We passed out our business cards to all the flight attendants and pilots who would take them. We broke the ice with every female we flew with by asking, *"Do you live here or do you commute?"* This was a perfect segway to talking about our crash pad for commuters, and even if they didn't need one for themselves, they usually knew someone who needed one.

I remember once when Angel and I were checking our mailbox in the Operations area, he noticed a girl lounging on one of the couches. In my hustle and bustle of early bird anxiety, I urged Angel that we didn't have much time to get to our gate; but his outgoing nature took over and he began talking to our colleague. She was a commuter but claimed that she really preferred co-ed crash pads because of their dynamic. We left her our card anyway, and I received a phone call from her about a month later. She was tired of sleeping on couches in Operations, and because she had already spoken with us, she felt comfortable in approaching us in her search. She claimed a spot with her deposit that same day.

It is also just as important that potential clients can reach you with ease. Clients want to do business with those who take them seriously, and who are willing to work with them. If I had not responded quickly to *Miss Co-ed Crasher*, she might have gone with another crash pad because she had just reached that point of "*I will not sleep in Ops anymore*", and was looking to resolve her problem right then and there. With a friendly phone call response and an invitation to visit, she was already obligated to consider making the commitment, and after seeing our lovely home, making conversation with some of our lovely girls, and getting comfortable at the dining room table with some hot tea in-hand, why would she really go anywhere else when she could simply... *stay*? I'm not saying that everyone works like this, but making the effort to understand each client's situation is certainly an advantage, and you'll never know if you're not at their fingertips. The lesson here is: *Network all the time and remain available to your potential clients as much as possible.*

## Check In!

In addition to my phone number (or Google number, which is free) and email address listed on the business cards, our Facebook page link is attached to each tear-off on our flyers, and I post regularly within Facebook groups where my market will see them. I keep up with posting flyers on bulletin boards where I can, such as at the training center, Facebook and Airport Operations areas. I check in and follow up with potential clients, even when someone tells me that they chose to go with another crashpad. Stand by, offer the education and your kindness, and you will find that often times the candidate will return to do business with you.

## Respond to Your Potential Clients!

When a potential client contacts me or submits an application, I make a point to respond with a phone call in a timely manner, within an hour or two if at all possible, with the goal being within 24 hours at the very latest. This punctual engagement in communication conveys professionalism, accessibility, availability, and thoughtfulness. You wouldn't want a landlord who places little importance on responding to you, would you? Contacting them quickly and with a friendly tone gives them a taste of what life will be like as one of our crashers, and moreover will provide me with a better idea of who *they* are, as well as encourage them to seal the deal with a deposit (*show me the money!*).

## Referrals & Reviews!

We formed a great relationship with our New Hire Mentors at base, who also sent us a few referrals. The beautiful thing about referrals is that we know the quality of candidate by who referred them. For this reason, we instituted a referral program, in which we give a $50 credit to the crasher who sent us a candidate who completes the application and stays with us for at least 90 days. Happy clients are personally asked to leave reviews for us at Crashpad411 and on our Facebook page- a small, short-term investment for a long-term, positive reputation.

## Review and Application

*If you can't sell your crash pad, running your crash pad will be pointless! Now, let's consider how we are going to promote your business and recruit new clients.*

1. **Give your crash pad a name!**
   a. How does the title fit your target audience and express what you're offering?
2. **Don't forget the visual appeal!**
   a. Create or hire someone to create a professional logo.
   b. Design flyers!
   c. Design and order business cards
   d. ...and mentally prepare yourself for handing them out to everyone!
3. **Social Media!**
   a. Highlight your amenities, perks and include your location.
   b. Include photos of your crash pad.
   c. Set up a contact form that will send inquiries to you, in the form of an organizational form (in our case, we used an excel document).
   d. Set up a CrashPad411 profile, complete with a description and photos of your crash pad.
   e. Request that guests who have visited or stayed at your crash pad leave a positive review on your profile and website.
4. **Network, Network, Network!**

a. Talk to everyone!
   b. Always carry business cards with you.
   c. Be available as much as possible to your potential clients.
5. **Check In!**
   a. Post within groups of your target audience on Facebook.
   b. Post flyers to bulletin boards where potential clients will see them.
   c. "Check in" whenever there's a fun event or news about your crash pad.
6. **Respond to Your Potential Clients!**
   a. Contact inquirers promptly.
   b. Use a friendly tone.
   c. Try to get an idea of who the person is.
7. **Referrals & Reviews!**
   a. Make friends with those who will often refer clients to you!
   b. Consider offering a perk for referrals and reviews.

# Chapter 6: The Application Process

Once an interest wants to become a client, and that they are ready to reserve their spot, the next question of course is ...*what's next?* In the last year, Angel and I have run through our application with a fine-toothed comb. It's important to display professionalism throughout the process and to *set your expectations* as clearly as possible to avoid misunderstandings later. Finally, you must use your best judgment of character, and your best-worded contract, reviewed and approved by an attorney, to *protect yourself*.

These are the steps we've created:

## *1. Candidate applies.*

We direct all potential crashers to our application form. Created via Google documents by my wonderful Angel, the application is available on our website, flyer, Crashpad411 profile, and Facebook page. All traffic is directed here, whether she has spoken with me directly or sent a message online. This not only proves her interest to us, but provides us with details we like to have in our decision-making process, including whether or not she has a car, if she's looking for a temporary place to stay or more of a long-term commuter situation, and for what date she's requesting a spot. There's an additional space to provide two references, along with their contact information. Everything on this form provides me with the information I need to compare with my *Projections* spreadsheet, to make sure we are even able to accommodate her request, to start the process of checking references, and to assist her in reserving a spot!

## 2. Touch base with the Candidate (Informal Interview).

Once I have received and looked over the application, I contact the candidate. I usually prefer to make a phone call (unless I'm out of the country, in which case I send an email or text). During the phone call, I listen to their tone of voice and wording and obtain a sense of character. I ask them to tell me a little about themselves, and I explain the next steps. *Trust your gut!* If something seems off about them, or they don't seem very friendly, or interested in the crash pad, they probably aren't a great fit. If they aren't flexible or understanding about the way in which your crash pad works, or they try talking you down in price, then they don't understand the value of your pad and they probably won't be very understanding of the other crashers once they move in, which could lead to problems in the future.

Here are some questions I typically ask potential crashers:
What's your situation? (Listen, and evaluate their energy and friendliness within the conversation).

Where are you commuting from? (It's a great sign if they have children and a house; they will *want* to go home as much as possible. In this part of the conversation, I also state the commuter rules to ensure they understand our expectations).
(After providing a description of the crash pad, including the awesome amenities...), "do you have any questions for me?"
(If they haven't already included them in their application...) "Are you able to provide two references for whom you've previously lived with? (If so, great! Ask them to send those over for a faster processing, and to reserve their spot -with a refundable deposit- more quickly).

This phone call is also your opportunity to hit home on the rules that are most important to you. I always reiterate the refundable deposit, which requires 30 days' notice provided via the Notice form. I let them know what our expectations for belongings at the crashpad are as well.

I once had such a difficult time communicating with a potential client after two weeks of back and forth via text, no replies for days and sudden requests to tour the pad, without any consideration for my schedule or time. During our second phone conversation, she told me that she was "in the car with a friend, driving somewhere" and that she would return my phone call. Completely understandable if she was the one driving. That phone call never came, and after a few days, she texted that she was in town and wanted to see the pad. I finally told her that she didn't seem very interested and that the spot was no longer available. Better to not waste my time on someone who isn't serious nor excited about my awesome product. *If she doesn't display communication skills now, why would that change once she becomes a paying customer?*

I also experienced a situation in which the crasher pleaded with me to lower the rate. I agreed to give her a discounted rate for the first three months, assured that she would appreciate the offer, fall in love with our location and stay. Instead, she only stayed for the three months, and then left at the three-month mark. She was only looking for the cheapest, and not necessarily the best, deal. *You don't want clients who aren't willing to pay full price for your product because they won't see the value of it.*

Lastly, if you don't get a great feeling after speaking with the potential client, or if the potential crasher is rude to you in your first time speaking with them, don't be afraid to call them back later and let them know that the spot is no longer available. There's absolutely no sense in allowing someone you don't feel good about to invade the great atmosphere you have created. *The crashers you obtain will become part of your product. And no one wants to be part of a drama-filled, negative space!*

## 3. Check References.

Although we know that the crew member has already passed a thorough a background check, I ask the candidate to provide two references of whom they have previously lived with (name and phone number). Our only exception is that if she has been referred by one of our crashers, she may skip this process, or I may ask for just one reference. Whenever I call my references, I mention who I am calling about, I ask them to tell me a little bit about the person, and what their experience was like living with them. I let them elaborate, and I listen for keywords: flexible, clean, respectful, friendly, courteous, considerate, etc. I wrap it up by explaining that there are a number of other girls in and out of the crash pad and ask if they have any reservations about their candidate staying there. I haven't turned anyone down yet based on references, and I believe it is because those who don't have great references aren't motivated enough to apply with us. I feel that only those who care enough about being in a more selective crash pad will be eager enough to send in references.

## 4. *Invoice & Agreement.*

Once references have been checked out, I let the candidate know, usually with a text. I let them know when they should expect the invoice and agreement (whenever I'm able to put their info into the system and makeup and send their agreement), and I mention that their spot will be reserved as soon as the deposit is made. Then, I add the client to my invoicing database, create the invoice, and send it along. I then modify the agreement template, attach and then send with a welcome email. I encourage them to read the agreement thoroughly and to download GroupMe as their move-in date approaches. If I didn't make it clear in the text or phone call, I mention that their spot will be reserved once the invoice is paid.

We *include the refundable deposit* on all of our invoices, to be returned when thirty days are provided before move-out. We've kept the deposit low because our market includes many new hires who aren't making more than 20k each year, but yet we needed to put something in place to encourage the courtesy of giving us the time to plan around each person's leaving. In August, two girls provided three days' notice, and one provided none at all. This left us with just a few days to replace the girls, and no time at all to replace the crasher who left without a word. And because we didn't know they would be leaving, we hadn't been actively recruiting crashers into the application process. It all worked out okay, and we were able to replace all of them, but we learned the simple lesson of requiring a small deposit in exchange of making sure that situation doesn't arise again.

We also include a disclaimer that all spots are reserved on a first-come-first-served basis.

## *5. Collect Money & Signed Agreement.*

*Don't ever hold a spot without payment to secure that spot.* Several times in the past, a potential client has guaranteed me that they will be taking a specific bed within the crash pad-even supposed friends- and have bailed out at the last minute. It's much less stress on you, and your wallet, for you to stick to this rule. After all, it's business, and we are in this to make money.

The signed agreement is important too and required before every client's arrival to the crashpad. I've never had anyone that was unwilling to sign the agreement.

## The Agreement.

It would be a great idea for you to consult a lawyer. While crash pads are appealing to commuters due to the lack of commitment required, I still require clients to sign an agreement so that everyone is in line with what is allowed and what's not allowed at the pad, which also happens to be my home. A great lawyer friend of mine looked over and officialized all of the language within our contract, and we still find ourselves adding and modifying expectations within the document regularly.

Following are some must-haves to include within your contract:

A statement that outlines criteria for using the pad.

A statement that spells out that Crasher has a primary residence, that they are not a tenant, and not liable to the property state code. They are not to be at the crash pad more than "X" number of days per month.

*Our number of days is sixteen.* We decided that crashers shouldn't be there more than half of the month, and probably wouldn't be anyway, between their schedules and going back to their *primary residences*. We also include a clause about leaving the pad if they have more than two days off in a row, to prevent clients from moving in.

Of course, there are always exceptions to every rule. One of our crashers hurt her foot once and was placed on the sick list for about a week, which meant that she was unable to fly home. She nervously asked me if she needed to pay additional rent for that month, but I assured her that we understand things happen, and would not charge her anything extra. It was the ethical thing to do, and made her a happier Crasher, after all.

There's a spot to initial that they understand and agree to the rate we offered them.

A list of house rules and expectations

Statements that forbid males, pets, and drugs at the crash pad property.

Agreement that the owner may ask the crasher to leave for any reason at any time.

Stipulations about late payments and fees.

*Although we have never exercised this, and have permitted a one-time late payment without fees to each Crasher, this discourages late payments and protects you in case you ever need to implement the charge.*

We require every client to sign up for Remind, a free app that places them into a class/group which I can send messages to. This is how I share the updated door codes in one simple step, from my phone. I also use this tool to announce important reminders whenever it deems necessary.

Candles and open flames are not allowed at my crashpad at any time. *Yes, someone once left a candle burning in her room. I almost had a heart attack!*

Parking should be addressed as well. Angel's designed a lovely parking map, using a little help from Google Maps, which we've placed on the client dashboard and plastered on the back of the front door as well. While we have a wide driveway and great curb parking, I've had to step up the education with new girls who have cars. I realized this was a greater need when one of them parked in an alleyway, blocking a neighbor in their driveway. This is one of the reminders that I send out as a Remind message every so often.

<u>Expectations about cleaning up after themselves</u>

*...including dishes and leaving items within common areas.*

Every client initials that they understand that our crashpad is NOT a hotel and that items left in common areas will end up in the lost and found box after 30 days.

*You've got to have a rule regarding dishes and clean up.* I told the maid from the very beginning, to *NEVER* wash anyone's dishes since I felt that would perpetuate laziness. We implemented a *"wash your dishes within twenty-four hours of use"* rule, only to be annoyed at the dishes left in the sink for up to those twenty-four hours after use. Some of the girls slowly filled the dishwasher before running it, which took a long time for each load, since Crashers aren't at the pad for very long periods of time. This may have sufficed had we not lived *in* the same crash pad we're running, but this was something that I could not tolerate. We finally adopted a *"clean your dishes by hand, immediately after use"* policy, and began providing paper plates and plastic cups, as an added convenience, and to discourage more dishes in the sink.

Crashers agree that they will not eat, drink or store food of any kind within the bedrooms, or on the couch. This invites critters, which upsets other crashers, disturbing the environment and can become very expensive. Two reports or complaints of someone eating in the bedroom results in the loss of deposit refund.

Information about how to assist in taking out the trash is listed on the agreement alongside rules about tying up loose items in trash bags. *I know, you would think a lot of this stuff would be obvious.*

We also include a commitment that clients will not flush anything down the toilet that is not toilet paper or human waste. We've still encountered many major plumbing issues anyway.

Visitor's rules and visiting hours

*We limit our visitors to 30 minutes or less.* We originally thought it was an unspoken rule to have visitors over for a long period of time. However, one of our Crashers brought a visitor into the living room one day, where they stayed, chatting until 3 A.M. The way we see it, there are already too many girls under one roof, and we don't need any more new people brought into the mix. Plus, most of the girls expressed their discomfort with the situation and felt that more than an hour was inappropriate.

Deposit Refund Guidelines

A clause that displays compliance of thirty days' notice before moving out, and that otherwise their deposit will be forfeited.

We recently started charging a *refundable deposit* from Crashers, after several ladies up and left without providing any notice whatsoever, and leaving me in a rush to fill the spot. I understand that flight attendants make chump change paychecks, but we ask for just enough to help them remember the policy. And if they don't, then hey, we're covered for a few days while I find a replacement, and I have a window of time before the lack of notice affects our potential profit. *Protect yourself!*

<u>Clearly defined storage limit</u>

An understanding that the Crash Pad is for their roller board suitcase, and anything additional that can be put underneath their bed, or in a designated closet space. There need to be specific hard limits on everything, including hangers allowed in the closet.

We once hosted a crasher that was a mess, *literally*. Looking back, we think that she was living between the crash pad and her boyfriend's apartment, leaving her with no storage other than her car. She brought in several huge suitcases, which came to my attention by the complaints of other crashers. Hence, this rule was born. Sometimes this rule is stretched, but only when all of the girls sharing the room are completely comfortable with someone's plastic organizer at the foot of their bed, or whatever.

Requirement that all Crashers label their food items.

*This helps us maintain organization, and helps prevent theft. We provide storage freezer labels in the kitchen for this purpose.*

During our first couple of months, our full-time roommate was very upset when she noticed someone had drank from her bottle of Fireball whiskey *(and I don't blame her!)*. From that moment, we placed a note on the fridge and adopted a *"zero tolerance for theft"* policy, which is outlined in the agreement for every new crasher to make note.

If you have any pet residents, you definitely want to include expectations regarding them.

One day, I was crouched over the dining room bar with Kate, picking at the leftovers from the previous days' Fiesta Night. Amie, my pup, pranced around us, hopeful that something would be dropped her way. Kate grabbed a piece of avocado and dropped it on the floor. "DON'T LET HER EAT THAT!!! NO, NO, NO!!" I screamed. As she picked it up off the floor and apologized, I gently explained to her that avocado is, in fact, poison for dogs; Amie once ate a small piece and had diarrhea for three days. We are n*ever* going through that again. So that was all it took to establish the next rule: *Do not feed Amie people food.*

We do not tolerate candles or open flames of any kind within the house. We once had a crasher who left a religious candle burning on the headboard of her bed. Not only do I have anxiety about open flames, having personally experienced a house fire, but it's just not safe! The agreement is your opportunity to object to whatever you are not comfortable with and ensure that every crasher will comply with those expectations.

An understanding that washer and dryer use equals one to two dollars in the tip jar, for power use and extra water. You might decide to include this service in your rate or to place a tip jar in hopes that everyone will be honest and contribute.

Agreement and acknowledgment of thoroughly reading the Welcome Packet

Our Welcome document includes common questions that one might have about the house, originally created to limit the repeat questions we were getting from Crashers. We covered the following topics: *Payment Options, Transportation, WIFI password, How to Use the TV, Transportation Talk, Location of Toilet Paper,* and *Things To Do Nearby.*

In case of Emergency contact information
*Just in case, because you just never know.*

Vehicle information (if applicable)

Waiver, Assumption of Risk, Release of Liability

*Finally, have a lawyer write this up for you, and look over your contract as well, to include any specific language that may better protect you.*

## Review and Application

*Here's what we've gathered over much time and effort to find what works best to recruit the best clients, ensure they understand the expectations and to protect the business!*

***The Application Process:***

1. **Candidate Applies.**
    a. Create an application form that gathers info you need, and direct all of your marketing and advertising there.
2. **Touch base with the candidate (Informal Interview).**
    a. During your phone call, pay attention to tone and wording, and try to get a vibe for the person's character. Ask the candidate to tell you about themselves.
    b. Ask pertinent questions, such as the points covered within this chapter.
3. **Check References.**
    a. Call the candidate's references.
    b. Listen!
4. **Invoice & Agreement.**
    a. Send along the agreement and first invoice for payment!
    b. Ensure that your agreement is proofed by a lawyer and that it reflects your expectations.
    c. Collect the signed agreement and deposit from the client!
    d. Update the *Projections* spreadsheet!

# Chapter 7: You Will Fail

I have so titled this chapter the undesirable but necessary truth that it is. It's best to understand that at some point, no matter how well-intentioned or hard working, or how much you thoughtfully laid out the framework, your plan will be executed only to crash and burn.

### *Identify your failures (or need for improvement).*

One of our greatest challenges was the transportation available. We attempted to maintain a crashpad car until we were discouraged by all of the issues it brought about. From clients taking advantage and abusing the car privileges, ensuring a process that was fair to everyone involved, to the petty drama that often comes along with multiple people sharing one vehicle. The final straw were both the girls who went joy riding around the city and the speculation that one of our clients had previously drank alcohol before getting behind the wheel. All of the stress of this outweighed the benefits of it.

Maintaining a clean fridge with enough space in a shared community also proved to be quite challenging. Thanks to freezer labels, we can easily keep track of what belongs to whom. At one point, freezer labels ran out and the maid cleaned out absolutely everything. Many groceries were tossed and crashers were upset. This was before the supplies request form, and completely my fault. I admitted failure and reimbursed those clients for the items thrown away. Furthermore, I ordered several pizzas to the crash pad and send out an apology. It was an expensive mistake, but nonetheless, there were options and we addressed the situation the best we could. Thanks to our wonderfully efficient maid, the fridge is now cleaned out once at the end of every month (except for condiments) and supplies are ordered via Prime Subscriptions. This is the best system we've come up with.

## *Address your failures, devise a plan, and execute.*

There have certainly been many failures in our time managing the crash pad. We learned and improved, and we are constantly improving. Issues and challenges arise, but there's always a solution to each one! What I hope stands out to you here is that *sometimes you fail, and when you do, you must brush yourself off, get back up and find a better way.*

## *Feedback and Reviews.*

Since we began in crash pad management, we've found how equally important it is to inspire feedback from our clients. In the beginning, we sent out surveys, but very few of the crashers completed them. The reviews left by crashers on their way out certainly provide an honest opinion of our pad, and we strive to consider and address every piece of input that we receive.

We are still, at the end of the day, very proud of the lessons we've learned through our failures as we navigate through the management experience. We've learned a lot, and are constantly improving. We pay just as much attention to negative feedback as we do positive feedback, if not more so. This is because we can not only hear what we are doing right, but also highlight those positive perks for potential clients (by word of mouth, on social media, within our Crashpad411 profile, and on our website), therefore improving our brand and reputation. When we make improvements, we make sure that our crashers notice, so that they sense that we are listening to them, and are constantly making efforts to improve their experience. This in itself improves the crash pad experience, but also, we ensure they notice because we know that flight attendants LOVE to talk. As they say, *if you want to keep a secret, don't tell your secret to a flight attendant.* On the flip side, if you wish for news to travel far, absolutely, most definitely, tell a flight attendant!

Whenever we receive compliments from crashers, we always tell them, "go write that in a review for us!" When we first started this business, we offered $5 gift cards to crashers for writing a review for us; and the positive branding was completely worth the investment. Now we can lead interested clients to our website, with the confidence of knowing that the reviews, images, and professionalism of the site will do half of the selling for us.

## *Celebrate Your Successes!*

Lastly, what I want to say about crash pad management is that it's very hard and never-ending work- but the flexibility and freedom of it has also enabled me to work remotely most days; I've found myself traveling through Europe and dancing to the beat of my own drum. But running a business is a beast of its own in the sense that if you're not careful you could fall into a never-ending pit of work if you let it. Don't forget to set business hours for yourself, and don't reply to clients outside of those hours. And, please take a moment for yourself once in a while to turn off your phone and have a glass of wine, clear your mind, and appreciate how far you've come.

# Review and Application

*While it may be difficult to recognize and accept your failures, remember that every failure is an opportunity to grow!*

1. **Identify your failures (or need for improvement).**
    a. Consider common complaints.
    b. What could help you get more clients?
    c. Is there anything about the business that currently feeds your stress level, and/or adds more work than is necessary?
2. **Address your failures, devise a plan and execute.**
    a. Compile a list of your greatest issues and need for improvement.
    b. Discuss the issues and devise a plan with the help of your team, or someone who may be able to offer a plan or solution.
    c. You always have options!
    d. If the solution is unclear, you may want to write out a cost-benefit analysis.
    e. Once you've decided on a plan, set the expectation and carefully communicate the developments with your clients.
    f. Carry out the plan, and follow up on how the plan plays out. Adjust as necessary.

3. **Feedback and Reviews.**
    a. Take the time to talk with and listen to clients.
    b. Read all reviews left on all public forums and profiles.
    c. Share improvements & developments with clients, which improves your brand.
4. **Celebrate Your Successes.**

# Chapter 8: Transportation

This topic deserves its own chapter because although I touched on this in the last chapter, it is probably the most important single factor to consider when making plans to start a crash pad. Unless commuters aren't traveling very far, most of them will not have their own car and are looking for a cheap way to get back and forth. Our competitors, the surrounding area hotels, usually provide shuttle service free of charge. *So, what kind of transportation can you offer?*

## *Community Car.*

When Angel offered up his car to the crashers, we truly had no idea what we were jumping into. We managed a GroupMe chat where every car user would post when they left the car, when they needed a ride (*because the last person to use the car would be responsible for picking up the next person*), and when the driver was on their way to pick up. We had a system for hiding the key *on* the car itself, and we created rules in contract form about how the car was to be used. We asked for copies of driver's licenses and insurance for each driver. We did everything we could to keep the process organized. This process would work smoothly, in theory. In reality, Angel and I felt like parents, always having to monitor the chat group, and making sure everyone was fulfilling their role responsibly. When we were out of town, we stressed about all the potential outcomes, including but not limited to: *What if someone wrecks the car? What if someone drinks and drives? What if one of the girls misses a trip because one of the others didn't wake up to take her? What if the car breaks down and we aren't there to fix the situation?* You get the point.

Our first phase simply required the girls to fill up the tank as necessary. *The problem?* The more generous girls were taken advantage of by others who never filled up the tank at all. In our second phase, we placed a gas card in the glove compartment, where anyone could fill up the tank as needed, the total being divided equally among each of the drivers, and paying every month for their use. *The problem?* Some of the girls abused the car, driving it far into downtown, sticking their cost of gas onto the rest of the girls. We pushed on and into our third phase, in which we charged a flat fee from each of the girls who used the car, and then we covered the gas bill. *The problem: what do we charge our senior crashers who never messed things up for anyone, and who are barely at the pad since they have mastered the art of commuting? And what does that fee cover? And will we always be able to cover the expenses of gas and maintenance with those monthly payments, or will we have to accept a loss at some point?*

Furthermore, we *never* came out on top, after the car payment, insurance, and maintenance, not to mention the wear and tear on the car (*and how do you calculate that?*). Crashers aren't interested in paying more than $35 per month for a shared car in which they are responsible for picking up and driving other girls at the pad too. We became fed up and stressed out whenever one crasher would fail another, whether they had slept through their notification or the entire group got mixed up in who was responsible for picking up who. Perhaps this system might have worked out better with a different group of people, but keep in mind that we had cycled through many crashers over the course of our existence, and nothing seemed to work well. While it was a great way to get crashers in the door when we first started the crash pad, we were losing money by having the crash pad car. For us, the stress and hassle was not worth it either. We tried for a better part of a year, before tossing in the towel and getting rid of the car. And we have been able to enjoy our vacations *A LOT* more since we did!

While we don't recommend it if you decide to provide a crash pad car, have car users put down a deposit first, and to sign a contract which details how you wish for them to use the car and how to handle situations that might occur. You should also obtain insurance that will cover a number of persons driving your car (the people who use the car will change often).

### On Call Shuttle Driver.

When we phased out the crash pad car, we began collaborating with Allen, a Lyft driver in the area who was opening his own transportation company.

We asked him to set flat rates for the girls, which he did and provided his number to the girls for scheduling pick up and drop off times. In theory, this should have worked out impeccably. The crashers paid Allen directly, communicated with him, and *he* was given the responsibility of getting the girls where they needed to be. *Stress shifted off of us!* It worked out well for the first month, but then we noticed some issues. He became too casual with the girls, and furthermore, he started showing up late! *Just typing that sentence makes me fume, as half of our job is showing up on time! For flight attendants on probation, usually within their first six months, being late could get them fired!* When one of our senior crashers got a missed trip due to his failure to be punctual, we removed his information from our website and stopped marketing his business to our clients.

In theory, this would have been the perfect solution and could have benefitted everyone involved if the right person were to fulfill the position. In fact, the only crash pad we ever lost crashers to was one that offered transportation around the clock. Apparently, the house was paid for, so the costs were lower than ours, and the family managing this pad worked in shifts to provide airport shuttle service. *Genius, if you have an entire family working for you, and are able to keep overall costs low.*

At this point, Lyft and Uber services seem to be the most reliable options, other than nearby public transportation. If you aren't familiar with these, they are both a rideshare service that operates through an app. Download the Lyft app and use the code TARA660 to try your first ride free. Sign up for Uber using the code "2h069" to receive $5 off your first two rides.

*If you ever find someone who is reliable, professional and punctual, and who is willing to provide transportation for your pad, I would recommend you jump on the opportunity to collaborate with them!* It could be a fruitful endeavor for both parties.

## *Public Transportation.*

The location of a crash pad makes all the difference, especially if the pad is directly on a line of public transportation. When we opened our second crash pad, we found a house just feet away from a bus route with a direct shot to the airport. This has been the best solution by far, as crashers can be independent without paying expensive fares, and without ever needing to involve the crash pad manager at all! While I also think that a shuttle driver would be useful to take crashers to and from the airport terminal, public transportation provides them with a lower cost and the freedom to get around and see the area. Many of the new hire flight attendants come out of *unpaid* training flat broke, so the less money they spend commuting to base, the happier they will be!

# Review and Application

*Please consider the following transportation options for your crash pad:*

1. **Community Car**
    a. Not recommended!
    b. Consider accountability of the entire group.
    c. How will you cover overhead costs?
    d. Consider insurance for all drivers.
2. **On Call Shuttle Driver**
    a. This option is beneficial for all parties.
    b. Collaborate with drivers who are punctual and professional.
    c. Don't get involved with payments or logistics.
    d. Consider Lyft and Uber, if available in your area.
3. **Public Transportation**
    a. Location makes all the difference!
    b. Offers lower fares and more freedom.
    c. Promotes independence and doesn't require *you* to manage the process!

# Chapter 9: Client Relations

*Keep Your Clients at a Distance!*

Some of the girls have been easy to keep at a distance. Laura, for instance, whose tone ranged from high to low in a matter of seconds, always over-analyzing something that didn't require the energy she put into thinking, questioning and panicking about. I viewed her as an annoying little sister more than anything, knocking at my door for random bits of advice, or simply to blab blab blab until we gracefully escaped. Drama seeped out of her pores, in a way that I could usually stand back, enjoy the entertainment for what it was, and laugh.

One morning, I awoke to a shrieking scream. Thinking something was terribly wrong, I jumped out of bed and ran out of my room. Laura was pacing throughout the house like a mad woman. Every few minutes, she would stop, throw her hands up hysterically, and shake them while she screamed. The few girls in the house could only stare at the five year-old-like tantrum, one of them helping to rummage through Laura's luggage, sprawled out on the dining room floor. I asked Karen what was wrong with her. "Ohh, she can't find her car keys," she said with a Nashville drawl. I thought back to the previous night when some of the girls were sharing wine and wondered if that had anything to do with it. "When is her sign in?" I asked and was informed that she wasn't due in at the airport for another three hours. The girls trying to calm her down only received snips from Laura about how she needed *HER KEYS* because *SHE WAS DRIVING.... Because THAT IS WHY she has a car!* She even began accusing another girl of taking her keys who had left earlier that morning. Finally, she agreed to let Angel and I drive her to the airport. But the next day, one of the girls sent me a photo of Laura's keys, placed firmly in the keyhole of her own trunk, where she had left them. I burst into laughter right there in the middle of boarding. *This is my life*, I thought. *I tell you this story so as to caution you and encourage you to create firm boundaries with your clients, otherwise, you'll be pulled into more drama than is necessary.*

Most of the girls who have come and left without issue did just so. There are only a handful who we have sincerely enjoyed and made lasting friendships with, most of whom we have been able to hold onto, and would sacrifice more than they realize in order to keep them. Jenny gave the sky life a try for six months, before moving to South Dakota to be with her boyfriend. All of the girls who knew her still bring up the fact that they miss her quirkiness, jokes, and laugh- and I for one, miss the ease of dealing with her as a client, too. We remain in touch to this day, and I've even served as a reference on applications she's submitted. Jenny signed up with us for twelve months but leaving after six, I should have technically kept her deposit- but I didn't need to, and didn't feel that it was the *right* thing to do. *Sometimes being ethical means bending the rules to accommodate awesome clients and wonderful attitudes. And guess what? She left us a raving review!*

And then there are some clients who, by nature, seem to nitpick about every detail, who always have questions about *this* or *that*. These are the girls who will make you lose your mind from time to time, will sometimes hate you forever, and will inspire a *deep* appreciation for your own space if you have it.

### Avoid Living in the Crash Pad.

We could have avoided so many issues had we not lived in the crash pad (*if only our finances would have allowed us to move out sooner!*). At one point, the dynamic shifted and our parent-like presence seemed to make the other girls a little uncomfortable. I think that the girls, having more in common (single, usually younger, living out of their suitcase, not owning a home or running a business, and most of the girls living paycheck to paycheck) found a groove while we were away, and when we came back to the house, our dominant, law-enforcement-like vibe interfered with that atmosphere. I imagine that this might be equivalent to living with a work supervisor. And it took a toll on us, always trying to be the example, setting rules, laying down the law, striving to be an acquaintance to the girls, and trying *not* to get too wrapped up in their personal lives- and then *constantly* being around at that. Because we lived with them, some of the girls thought that we *were* friends, and took advantage of that, assuming it was okay to make late payments. I usually give one freebie, but then enforce the late fee the following time, unless there's an extreme circumstance. It was extremely difficult to get away from the business when we *lived in the business.* Perhaps we kept a better eye on things, but we sure didn't enjoy getting told on the way to the shower that there's a mold issue on the carpet, or to hear about one girl's dislike for another, while trying to make a pot of coffee. *No one* should have to deal with business before having a cup of coffee, in my opinion.

I would much prefer to be the fair landlord who the crashers never really think about until the first of the month (*when payments are due!*), who contact me with complaints during business hours. Additionally, all of the things we use to live our daily lives create a sort of clutter where there otherwise wouldn't be, and the things we value using every day aren't things we want the crashers to use. Living spaces and crash pads don't mesh well, for everyone involved. *I highly suggest that, in any way possible, you avoid living in the crash pad.*

## Don't Allow Crashers to Live in the Crash Pad.

Before we enforced too many restrictions or expectations, before we didn't know all the right questions to ask, we accepted two ExpressJet flight attendants. The two new hires were on a constant reserve schedule, which meant they needed to use the crash pad more than the other crashers, who typically had reserve schedules every *other* month. While the ladies listed primary residences on their application form, they obviously had no intentions of living anywhere else other than the crash pad. The girls spread their luggage across the room, and they wouldn't leave unless they got called out for a trip. As a result, one of the girls became too comfortable, excessively occupied the couch and TV, and crossed a line with us when she demanded that everyone do the dishes her way, which required *a talk*. We finally advised both Express Jet girls that if they chose to continue their stay with us the following month, that they would be obligated to pay a higher rate since they were utilizing the crash pad much more than we had expected or agreed upon. The couch potato vacated the pad the next day, and her colleague left the next month.

We now offer *temporary* full-time rates on a case by case basis, which are reviewed at the end of every month. *By setting the expectation right away with incoming clients, we avoid a lot of hassle.*

## Bad Apples.

There will *always* be bad apples in every bunch- even in the airline industry, where applicants are background checked and intensely interviewed. Hopefully, your application process and reference checks will help to weed out those apples. Should a less than ideal crasher make their way into your crash pad, and your warnings and talks with them do not improve the situation, your agreement (*listing your expectations*) should protect you, should you ask them to vacate. Don't beat yourself up about it. If other crashers ask you what happened, try not to gossip, and just know that your crashers will most likely be understandable of your choice to terminate their agreement. *After all, your crashers are part of your product, and in order to provide the best atmosphere, you'll need the best clients!*

## Feedback & Word of Mouth!

If crashers feel they can approach you about problems, whether be it in person or anonymously, you will be able to resolve them more quickly, improving the quality of your pad! Not to mention, constant improvements and upgrades will not only keep your crashers happy, but the good news will travel fast- and next thing you know, *your crashers will become your greatest advocates and referrals*!

When we decided to upgrade each of the bunks, we carefully considered the needs of our clients. We knew that we had done a great thing when I received a phone call from one of our clients' crewmembers, telling me how excited she was to hear about our blackout privacy curtains! Our crasher had raved on and on about how much she loved crashing with us, and in turn, landed us two additional clients (her crewmember referred *her* friend!)! Don't ever think that your actions will go unnoticed! Your crashers will notice everything you *do* and *don't do*... And flight attendants *looooove* to talk. *If you address their wants and needs, not only will you make your clients happy, but by word of mouth, they will bring you even more happy clients!*

# Review and Application

*This section of the book is for your sanity! Keep the following in mind, and you'll thank me later.*

1. **Keep Your Clients at a Distance!**
   a. Create firm boundaries with your clients.
   b. Sometimes being ethical means bending the rules to accommodate awesome clients and wonderful attitudes.
2. **Avoid Living in the CrashPad.**
   a. No one should have to deal with business before having a cup of coffee in the morning.
   b. Living spaces and crash pads don't mesh well, for everyone involved.
   c. <u>Don't do it!</u>
3. **Don't Allow Crashers to Live in the Crashpad.**
   a. Set expectations right away with incoming clients.
   b. Set commuter and full-time rates if this is something you plan to offer.
4. **Bad Apples.**
   a. There will always be bad apples in every bunch.
   b. Your agreement should protect you should you ask a crasher to vacate.
   c. Your crashers are part of your product, and in order to provide the best atmosphere, you need the best clients!

5. **Feedback & Word of Mouth!**
    a. Listen to your clients.
    b. Happy clients bring you more happy clients.

# Chapter 10: Quality of Crash Pad Life

## *Security.*

At our front door, a keypad lock security system is installed and programmed with a code. We prefer this to creating numerous keys every month, obviously, but this also allows us to change the code whenever a crasher leaves. A motion-sensor light overlooks the front porch, where every client rolls their roller board in and out. Posted on the back of the front door are the parking map and a sign displaying photos of me and my team, and a reminder not to let anyone else into the house. We have a security system with cameras facing each entryway of the house, as well as the kitchen and living room. The security system was certainly an upgrade for me as a manager. It's great to have the ability to monitor the house from anywhere.

## *Set Up.*

Drawers and cabinets are labeled in the kitchen, and there is designated food storage for every bunk. Crashers use the permanent markers in the cup on the counter and the freezer labels to mark their personal items. A closet in the hallway provides for another storage space for client bath and shower supplies, within a caddy above a shelf, labeled with the corresponding bunk bed numbers. A sectional couch offers a comfortable place for several crashers to relax in the living room, equipped with a flat-screen TV, cable included, Netflix and various gaming systems *(in all honesty, they aren't played very much, but I think that potential crashers like to know that they're there)*. A laminated sign on the wall illustrates how the remote works. A custom-built bar and 7 stools offer adequate seating space in the dining room that looks out into the backyard. The backyard offers an additional space to enjoy the outdoors during nice weather, either in a chair, lounge bed, or a hammock nestled within the trees. An ashtray on the patio table clarifies where smokers should ash their cigarettes. Finally, part of the dining room was converted into an image room, an additional space where clients can change and get ready before a flight without disturbing anyone else in their room. A vanity and two mirrors line the wall, along with an image of Audrey Hepburn. Some bins on the wall hold a hair dryer, curling iron, hairspray, nail polish remover, and bobby pins.

Every room has a fire alarm and smoke detector. There is also a fire extinguisher in the kitchen.

We assigned a letter to each room, and a number to each bed, which has helped me significantly with the Projections sheet. Card placards are installed onto each bed, featuring the name of the crasher who occupies that bed; This has helped a lot in welcoming new crashers to their beds for the first time.

We started out with used bunk beds (*thanks to Craigslist*), and attached power cords and shelves onto the beds to offer the high-in-demand charging stations and a resting place for tablets and phones. Shower hooks are installed in each room, to keep the common bathroom orderly and without items cluttering up the space.

And then Matt came along, Angel's best friend from childhood and skilled carpenter. He's built furniture for years and remodels for fun. He has a keen eye for design and style. The custom built *Lux Bed* (*though, I did come up with the name!*) would have never been without his hard work and expertise. He bumped everything up a notch, including our price point. Built into the wall, these sturdy beds were built from scratch, sanded down and stained to accommodate adults. We measured the bottom floor space to ensure that flight crew could store their roller boards, with plenty of space. Each bed features a shelf, power port (installed directly into the wall, this time), a reading light and black-out privacy curtains. Crashers tell me that the curtains are so effective that another person could turn on the bedroom light, and the other girls would never even know it. They are *very* happy with the privacy curtains, and the Lux bed all around! I coined the term *Lux Bed* for these, which I like to think bumped up our marketing and reputation, as well. No one else in the entire area could offer the exclusive, superior *Lux Bed*!

## *Atmosphere.*

We encourage everyone to quiet down after 9 pm, and we take note when someone has a late arriving flight, or came in late from a trip the night before and probably needs the rest. There's a shelf in the dining room that holds about ten books, a small community library. We inspire community by offering food at the crash pad for Christmas. And *sometimes,* on holidays or *just because I had the opportunity to visit Anchorage,* I leave small tokens of "thanks for being our client" on everyone's pillow, usually in the form of chocolate.

References are huge for us. If someone we really like requests to have someone they really like come into our pad, then we figure they will be a great fit. We also find that in most cases, it elevates the quality of crash pad life for everyone. Of course, checking references in general assists in bringing in clients who are sociable, respectful, and get along with everyone.

I need to mention that the quantity of crashers affects the workload and environment. When I started with six clients, it only required a few minutes of my time every month to set up new clients and process payments. It wasn't demanding at all, and while I don't encourage crash pad apartments, I could see how easy it could be to simply offer 4 spots within a given room. I hardly saw any two people at one time. It was after ten people that my workload became more demanding, with more requests, applications, required cleaning, and keeping track of client invoicing. A billing system, the GroupMe chat group, two full bathrooms, maid service, my maintenance team, and checking supplies on the regular became a requirement at that point. I would absolutely recommend starting with a handful of crashers before expanding to accommodate an entire household. At fourteen crashers, our living full-time at the crash pad became an impediment to the crash pad environment and to *our* quality of life and privacy. And while this meant our crash pad was consistently full, two-four crashers would commonly be there at one time. Success, in this case, meant that the next logical step for us was to move out.

## *Weekly Household Responsibilities.*

I've compiled a list of weekly "to do" items that I consider requirements in maintaining a high quality of crash pad life that I hope you will find helpful!

- Sweep/mop all common areas and vacuum bedrooms.
- Wipe down common spaces.
- Clean showers and toilets.
- Clean out the fridge, and throw away what went bad.
- Put the trash out twice a week.
- Tidy up the common areas, and place missing items into the 'lost and found' box.
- Repairs and upgrades, as needed.
- Bed checks for food, drinks and to ensure labeled items do not exceed the limit.

- Yard work, as needed.
- Make appointments for repairs and maintenance as necessary.

- Amazon Prime Subscription orders for daily operation, such as:
    - Toilet paper
    - Paper towels (or recycle cloth dish rags)
    - Paper cups
    - Paper plates
    - Plastic silverware
    - Coffee
    - Freezer labels and markers
    - Cleaning Supplies
    - Trash can liners

## *Your Maintenance Team.*

As I've been told, you can't grow unless you learn to trust others. I suggest that you put together your maintenance team from the very first client. Instead of trying to do everything by yourself, consider outsourcing some things to professionals who will probably do the job better than you anyway. I highly recommend that you first acquire a trustworthy & experienced maid who will provide a thorough cleaning of the house every week. You will also want a reliable lawn service, and you may also want to hire out someone to take out the trash. Set up service with the most reliable pest control service you can find. *And absolutely* set up a home warranty if you don't have one already. Having a warranty will be a monthly cost, but I consider it an insurance. In my experience, it's always worth it just to have it and not need it, rather than need it and not have it! I can't tell you how many toilets we've had replaced – *and things always seem to break when we're traveling!* The backup of a home warranty has really come through for us on many occasions, sending their guys in as soon as we request it. Signing up for a home warranty at the very beginning will save you lots of money, time and stress.

# Review and Application

*A few things to consider regarding crash pad quality of life!*

1. **Security**
    a. Keypad door lock.
    b. Motion-sensor light.
    c. Security camera system.
2. **Set Up**
    a. Label storage spaces and cabinets.
    b. Markers and labels for labeling personal items.
    c. Equip your common areas with adequate seating and amenities.
    d. Fast Wi-Fi is a must!
    e. Set Up an Image Room.
    f. Install a smoke detector & fire alarm in each room, and fire extinguisher in the kitchen.
    g. Consider your version of Lux Beds!
3. **Atmosphere**
    a. It's the little things!
    b. Inspire community.
    c. References.
    d. Consider quantity of crashers.
4. **Weekly Household Responsibilities**
    a. Use the provided list to elevate the quality of life at your pad!
    b. Could you add to this list for your crash pad?
5. **Your Maintenance Team**

# Chapter 11: Money Matters

## *Money Matters.*

I'm sure you're wondering what the numbers look like. With a little math, you could roughly estimate profits and expenses that you're capable of.

The following graph illustration shows gross profits for 2 crash pads over the course of 15 months. One crashpad has 22 beds and the other crashpad has 14. The rates varied based on demand but stayed between $250 and $270 per month for each bed filled. This graph accounts for empty beds per month as well, so you will notice that the crashpads performed better on some months than others.

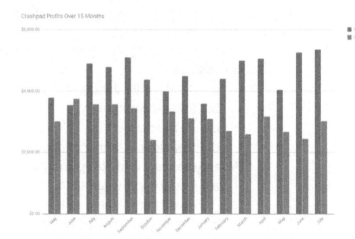

It is important to note that the above graph does not include expenses necessary for each crashpad to run smoothly. Many of your monthly bills are going to shoot up more than you'll ever see for a common household. There will be more water and sewer usage, more wattage, more breakage- more *everything*. I'm attaching a list of expense items I typically find in our monthly budget spreadsheet:

- Mortgage payment
- Maid/Cleaning service
- Electricity/Solar power
- Cable/WIFI
- Netflix Subscription
- Water Usage
- Trash
- Gas
- Warranty coverage/service
- Lawn service
- Waste management service
- Pest Control service
- Household Supplies
- Security camera system
- Marketing (Business cards, Google Ads, Crashpad411 subscription, flyers, etc.)

## *Seasons.*

Over the last four years in the crashpad and airline business, we've gathered some information that taught us some common trends in the industry. Just like any other business, we've noticed that there are certain months that do better than others. October is always a slower month. We believe that the airline stops hiring flight attendants around this time, which results in fewer flight attendants looking for a crashpad to commute to. We use these lulls of time in business to make improvements. Other times, we are flooded with applications and inquiries. You can also see the influx of crashpad business in the following graph for applications we received from 2014 through 2015.

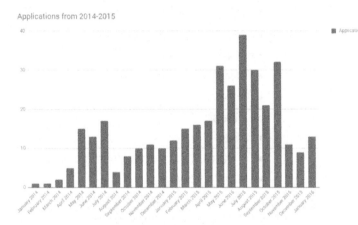

Applications from 2014-2015

## *Reporting Income.*

In my desire to grow and expand the crash pad business further, I was motivated to incorporate as a business. I also went this route so that I could write off every house-related purchase, and get a nice tax refund at the end of the year.

I began weighing out the risks. If I left the income unreported, I would need to rent a safe deposit box from my local bank and store the cash there. But it wouldn't be able to be invested into stocks or into the purchase of another house, and would eventually depreciate. Plus, *it is illegal.*

If I wanted to report the income, it would need to be through a proper business. After speaking with several trusted business owners, I learned more about the functioning of incorporated businesses and sole proprietorships. Bottom line, *the IRS wants us to report our income,* so they can tax it! By forming a sole proprietorship, I could report earnings for the *services* that I provide to airline crew, and I would also be able to deduct expenses acquired by my business.

I am fully aware that 99% of crash pads do not report their earnings and run their operation under the table, so I would like to share the experience of one man who I spoke with in a nearby town. His crash pad was shut down by the city he operated in because a neighbor reported him. The city gave him thirty days to kick out all but four crashers, based on city code, and to remove all marketing and advertising that he had posted. I'm not sure if the IRS ever came after him or not, but I just wanted to give you an idea of what might happen if you start your crash pad without the proper permission or following proper city code.

## *Back-Up Plan.*

I have contemplated if I truly wanted to expand to multiple crash pad properties in the future, given the incredible workload and energy that it requires. My original focus was to pay off the house, and once that happened, I decided that I would be happy to convert my house(s) into rental properties, and to deal with a lot less stress of the business, as Angel and I got older and would primarily be focusing on family. *This* was our back up plan for if the crash pad failed, anyway. We never really expected to expand the business over four years into one that would bring in more income than our full-time careers. We decided that even if our crash pad business went under one day, that we could always rent out the rooms to other crew members as roommates, and that would at least cover the mortgage.

Another type of airline crew property to consider are crew houses, where airline crew live. Even the full-time flight crew members often seek out living arrangements that don't require long contracts or leases, where furnishing is included and where the community is familiar.

Airbnb is another type of property management you may want to consider. Rates are set for nightly, weekly and monthly stays. Although it is not exclusive to airline crew, I have noticed that Airbnb properties nearby airports have can be successful if they are set up and managed well. I wouldn't recommend mixing Airbnb guests with airline crew, however. This is simply another route you could go, and a considerable back up plan for business.

## *Invest Wisely!*

During one of our flights, we were referred to a financial advisor who had assisted a fellow crewmember to grow their finances over many years. The couple now had four successful rental houses and had put their daughter through college. We were impressed and dreamed of the day we had more money to invest. We needed him to say this: *"You never have too little money to have a financial advisor!"* He advised us in a sweet but firm, fatherly tone, and we called up Ky the next day to set up an appointment.

Whether you decide to launch a crash pad or not, and whether it becomes an expanding business or stays small, I wholeheartedly believe that everyone should have a financial advisor to help them devise a path to their future goals and retirement. It worked out to just $40 a month- less than cable TV! Personally, it felt really great to lay it all down for him: the expenses, income, the 401K stuff I never look at, and every piece of the budget puzzle, to see exactly where we stood, and to be kicked in the butt to do what needs to be done to reach our ultimate goals.

While we're on the subject of investment, as more time passes and I acquire less time on this earth, I understand more and more that investment is not only financial but that it is time, energy, sometimes your social life, sore muscles, headaches, and sacrifice. I have offered up my experience in hopes that you will be able to make an informed decision, knowing what kind of investment is required to become successful in this niche. I hope that whatever you do, be it a crash pad or not, that your whole heart believes in the goal, and that you're willing to invest yourself 110%. Only then will you see your investment produce a great return.

# Review and Application

If you are planning to start and manage your crash pad as a business, you will need to consider the following.

1. **Money Matters!**
   a. Estimate potential profits and keep track of them.
   b. Consider all budget costs.
2. **Seasons.**
3. **Reporting Income.**
   a. *The IRS wants us to report our income*, so they can tax it!
   b. Form a sole proprietorship or LLC.
   c. Be aware of the risks if face if you choose to run your crash pad illegally.
4. **Back-Up Plan.**
   a. *Make sure that you have one!*
5. **Invest Wisely!**
   a. *You never have too little money to have a financial advisor!*
   b. Investment is not only about money.
   c. Invest yourself 110% in whatever you do.

# About the Author

Tara currently manages two successful crash pads, with the help of her amazing team- Angel, Matt and her father. When she isn't traveling, she enjoys spending time with her family, including her two dogs.

Stay up to date on the crash pad industry and be the first to know about Tara's next book by signing up for her newsletter:
Http://www.crashpadqueen.com

Made in the USA
Las Vegas, NV
31 December 2021